LEADING ADVISOR

SPOTLIGHTS ON REMARKABLE FINANCIAL PROFESSIONALS AND ADVISORS

LEADING ADVISOR

SPOTLIGHTS ON REMARKABLE FINANCIAL PROFESSIONALS AND ADVISORS

LEADING FINANCIAL PROFESSIONALS AND ADVISORS

FEATURING:

Clint Gharib

Mike Proctor

Christien Hughes

Abby Santiago

LM “Stamp” Stamper

Tony De Santis

John Nowicki

Keven Prather

Zachary Morris

Samantha N. Dinh

Remarkable Press™

Royalties from the retail sales of "**LEADING ADVISOR: SPOTLIGHTS ON REMARKABLE FINANCIAL PROFESSIONALS AND ADVISORS**" are donated to the Global Autism Project:

Global Autism Project

AUTISM KNOWS NO BORDERS;
FORTUNATELY NEITHER DO WE.®

The Global Autism Project 501(C)3 is a nonprofit organization that provides training to local individuals in evidence-based practice for individuals with autism. The Global Autism Project believes that every child has the ability to learn, and their potential should not be limited by geographical bounds. The Global Autism Project seeks to eliminate the disparity in service provision seen around the world by providing high-quality training to individuals providing services in their local community. This training is made sustainable through regular training trips and contiguous remote training. You can learn more about the Global Autism Project and make direct donations by visiting **GlobalAutismProject.org.**

Leading Advisor/ Mark Imperial —1st ed.

Managing Editor/ Shannon Buritz

ISBN: 978-1-954757-13-4

CONTENTS

A NOTE TO THE READER

Thank you for obtaining your copy of "LEADING ADVISOR: Spotlights on Remarkable Financial Professionals and Advisors." This book was originally created as a series of live interviews; that's why it reads like a series of conversations, rather than a traditional book that talks at you.

My team and I have personally invited these professionals to share their knowledge because they have demonstrated that they are true advocates for the success of their clients and have shown their great ability to educate the public on the topic of Financial Planning.

I wanted you to feel as though the participants and I are talking with you, much like a close friend or relative, and felt that creating the material this way would make it easier for you to grasp the topics and put them to use quickly, rather than wading through hundreds of pages.

So relax, grab a pen and paper, take notes, and get ready to learn some fascinating insights from our Leading Advisors.

Warmest regards,

Mark Imperial
Publisher, Author, and Radio Personality

INTRODUCTION

"LEADING ADVISOR: Spotlights on Remarkable Financial Professionals and Advisors" is a collaborative book series featuring leading professionals from across the country.

Remarkable Press™ would like to extend a heartfelt thank you to all participants who took the time to submit their chapter and offer their support in becoming ambassadors for this project.

100% of the royalties from this book's retail sales will be donated to the Global Autism Project. Should you want to make a direct donation, visit their website at GlobalAutismProject.org

CLINT GHARIB

CLINT GHARIB, AIF®, CFEd®

Conversation with Clint Gharib, AIF®, CFEd®

Clint, you are the Co-founder of Oxford Retirement Advisors. Tell us about your work and the people you help.

Clint Gharib: We're an independent financial firm. My partners and I left a larger firm quite a few years ago and started up this practice independently. Throughout my 32 year career in the financial services business, I've built multiple departments inside financial firms, advised other reps, clients, and families, and handled estates, trusts, and foundations. We realized we wanted to focus specifically on clients instead of building a large firm, so we have gotten smaller to get better, so to speak. We offer our services specifically to our investment clients, consisting of individuals, families, business owners, and foundations. We also work with many entrepreneurs designing investment, retirement, and income strategies.

What has changed for your clients as a result of the pandemic?

Clint Gharib: I don't know that anything has really changed in our planning. More people are making sure that they have plans when faced with a severe downturn like this. This pandemic is new for most of us, as opposed to stock market crashes or business cycles. But in any trying time, it seems to expose either those who didn't have any plans or plans that had a lot of holes without much detail. So I don't know that financial planning has changed. But I see more people saying, "Hey, we haven't discussed my plan in a while. Let's review it." I was always the one that had to initiate those conversations in the past. We have also seen more referrals come through the door. But certainly, people are more aware of their insufficient financial plans these days.

Are there any common myths or misconceptions that prevent people from getting their financial affairs in order?

Clint Gharib: Everyone is always worried about the next big crash, no matter where they are at in the cycle. It scares many people away from taking any action, and they get paralysis by analysis. That is a myth I have seen throughout my career, and the pandemic has exacerbated it. I've known people who've been sitting in cash for years now, waiting for the next crash, and they've missed out on one of the greatest bull markets we've seen over the past three years. Now, I'm not saying you should blindly rush into investments, especially stock investments. But I also don't like to see people not investing at all because of this doom and gloom mentality.

Another myth that's very common right now is that we are approaching financial Armageddon, and the dollar will crash. So you need to get anything that is dollar-related out. I've been hearing that throughout my entire career, off and on at different times. As they say, it's like a broken clock. It's right twice a day. In a frozen state of fear, you miss out, which causes more damage. If you had inched your way in slowly and it does drop, then great. You get to accumulate more.

On the other side, we have the people that came out of the pandemic wanting to play in meme stocks, with the idea they can get rich quickly. This year, you can point at a plethora of stocks with gigantic runs that are not typical. It's not normal to make a 100% return in six weeks. But we've seen that a lot in this past year, more so than any other time I can think of in recent history. And that fuels the other myth of people thinking the market can never go down. So you've got those who are afraid and then those on the other side of the coin who have never invested until the pandemic. They have never seen a down market, so in their minds, this is normal. Say they make an 8% return on something in a short amount of time. They think, "Oh, this is a terrible investment."

I always go back to the adage my grandfather taught me when I was a young kid. "Eight is great. Nine is divine." If you can make a 9% average annual return over a long period, that is historically the best of the market, right? 9% to 10% is the long-term historical average. So when we have a really good year, we need to think of it as a batting average. My son came home from school very excited the other day because he was five for five on hitting. And when I explained to him what a 400 batting average meant, he thought that was preposterous. Well, two days later, he came home, and he got one hit out of five; struck out four times. You have to apply the law of averages, not just consider one day. It's the same thing in the market. It's not just one year or one quarter. And people think it can't go down, especially with the new cryptocurrency trend and seeing huge percentages. Perhaps these myths have always existed, but they have been hugely exacerbated recently.

What is a meme stock?

Clint Gharib: People would get together and talk about certain stocks on social media and then collectively take action. So that is how it all started. It is now becoming an industry term for stocks that are moved due to a social media movement on a particular company.

What are some common mistakes you help people avoid?

Clint Gharib: One of the most common mistakes is involving mutual funds. They are the most widely used investment vehicle in this country, primarily because of 401Ks and retirement plans. People don't understand overlapping stocks. Let me explain. A mutual fund may have 100 different stocks and managers decide what to buy, when to buy, how much to sell, when to sell, etc. The first problem I see is that people pick their mutual funds based on track records. Looking at a five-year window, they will end up with a lot of the same funds investing in the same place. That is why they all have a successful record. When we review people's portfolios, we often see they have five or six different mutual funds, but they are all invested in the same area of the market. So when you really look at it, those five or six funds may only really be one or two different funds.

The second mistake is people take more risks than they should. And we see this A LOT. These are people who have saved their money, done very well, put a plan in place, but then we find they have a very aggressive portfolio in the market. Say, for example, to achieve their goals and lifestyle; they only need to make a 6% return. An overly aggressive plan could fall significantly and put them behind schedule if something goes wrong. So we encourage people not to take more risk than needed.

When we sit down with people for the first time who have not done any planning, their biggest mistake is often being overly conservative. They are the complete opposite. Their money is usually sitting in a hodgepodge of different accounts. And in almost all cases, too much of their money is in cash or very low-yielding investments that offer them no real upside potential return. They want to achieve specific goals, and there's no way they can get there with that type of allocation.

Clint, what inspired you to get into the financial services field?

Clint Gharib: It's funny because growing up as a child, this is not anything I would have thought I would be doing. In fact, even in college, I never would have thought this was what I'd be doing. My whole focus was on national security when I was a kid. So in college, political Science and Russian were my majors. After college, when I was trying to find jobs in my field, I had a friendship with a guy who worked for Shearson. I had a small amount of money that I had received from an inheritance, and he helped me invest it and taught me along the way. But when the crash of 1987 happened, I was in college. My mother and I had a small restaurant in Indiana, and prior to the stock market crash, we were in a real bind. And I've written a blog about the dangers of writing personal guarantees, which my mother and I learned the hard way being young entrepreneurs. But I had a decision to make right away; either use the money I had saved from working to put towards college for the next semester or use it to keep the family restaurant. So I had a real dilemma. When the crash happened, it was a bad day for many people. But for me, it changed my whole life. I ended up taking all the financial aid that I had for the next semester and all the money I had saved and went full into the stock market. I ended up doing so well with the recovery in a short amount of time that I could pay for my next semester AND help the family business. So in a sense, I went from one of the saddest moments of my life to getting everything I hoped for. Ever since then, I have looked at the stock market as a way of achieving dreams. I realize I got lucky though. And I would never advise people to take everything and go all in like I did. But from then on, my passion became investing and how to hedge risk. There are always opportunities in the market. And you hear media personalities saying there are bull markets and bear markets, and you can make money either way, right? And that's true. There's always opportunity; you've got to look for it. But it's all about how to hedge that risk.

After college, as I was waiting for different government job offers and security clearances, I got accepted into a training program with a financial firm. By the time my first government offer came through, I had excelled in the financial program so much that I turned down the government job. And when you turn down one, you aren't going to get offered more. But I took to the financial industry like a duck takes to water, and I never looked back. So here I am, 30 years later, helping people achieve their dreams through investing. And it's a great feeling when that happens.

What should people look for when choosing a financial advisor to work with?

Client Gharib: Don't take referrals from friends blindly. Your situation could be completely different from theirs. Even if you are the same age, have the same amount of money, and have the same goals, temperaments and personalities are different. You need to find an advisor that matches with you and makes you feel comfortable. But I would caution; make sure the person is a fiduciary and registered as an investment advisor. I'm not just a broker. And there's nothing wrong with being a broker, by any means. But there is a very different level of responsibility. A fiduciary is required by regulation to always put the client's interests first, in any circumstance, and if there's a conflict of interest, they need to make that known. So I would encourage you to work with someone who has that licensing. It's not a guarantee they will fulfill that duty, but at least it's another level of responsibility. And it should give you a little bit more comfort.

I would also say take a good look at how long they have been in the profession. One of my first clients told me, "The profession you are in is kind of like being the guy who puts horseshoes on a horse. You can study all day long and read all the books, but you have to get that horse in the straps. You have to be in it." Experience matters. If someone's never been through a bear market, if they've never been through a crisis or a crash in the market, then it's very different. It's like the old joke, "Everyone who fought Mike Tyson had a plan until they got hit the first time." It's the same way in the market. You need to make sure whoever you are working with has significant experience.

In addition, set up a meeting with them. Talk to them, spend time with them, and make sure they understand your situation. Determine whether or not what they are saying back to you makes sense. I would be wary of anyone with cookie-cutter proposals such as, "I have these models. Take this questionnaire to see what model you might fit." Well, that might work for some people, but I find that situations are as unique as the person.

Don't let cost be your only determining factor. Sometimes you get what you pay for, and other times you are being overcharged. But make sure to evaluate cost as one piece of the larger puzzle. Many times we meet with people who have no idea what they are paying their current advisor. When you hire an advisor, they become one of your essential employees. They work for you. So you should know upfront what you are paying and always feel free to ask as many questions or seek as much advice as possible.

How do people find you, connect with you, and learn more?

Clint Gharib: Our website is OxfordRA.com. My email and phone number can be found there. Not to mention, if you Google my name, I'm probably the only one you will find. Your best bet is the website where you can see our whole team, our approach, and read our past blogs and market updates to get a feel for what we do.

Are you 100% satisfied with your portfolio and the advice you're getting? If not, contact us for a free review and discussion.

CLINT GHARIB, AIF®, CFEd®

Co-Founder

Oxford Retirement Advisors

Clint is the founder and a senior member of Oxford Retirement Advisors. His life was forever changed when he was able to stay in college from gains made in the stock market, and he has had a passion for using the markets to accomplish dreams since then. Clint is an entrepreneur to the core and has appeared in or been quoted in media outlets such as Dow Jones Newswire, WSJ.com, Forbes, CNBC, and AJC.com. Clint graduated from Indiana University – Go Hoosiers! – with two Bachelor of Arts degrees in 1989. Mitigating risk has been and remains Clint's obsession which may be why many of his clients are other financial professionals. Only his faith, family, and love of the USA exceed his passion for managing portfolios.

WEBSITE: www.OxfordRA.com

PHONE: 404-479-8341

MIKE PROCTOR

MIKE PROCTOR, CFP®, RICP®

Conversation with Mike Proctor, CFP®, RICP®

Mike, you are the Founder of Leading Edge Financial Planning. Tell us about your work and the people you help.

Mike Proctor: Our work is centered on what we call "lifestyle financial planning." We focus on helping our clients get the most out of life in the time they have left, and that looks different for everybody. Specifically, we work with many retirees and business owners. About half of my personal clients are business owners. We work on assets under management base or subscription financial planning, which is a planning fee model that works great for business owners because most of their net worth is tied up in their business. We get into different types of valuations and work tactically with owners on how to grow their business. It's been such a rich experience, being able to work with our clients in a way that helps bring the most out of their finances. I love seeing people being able to balance goals and objectives, put their families first, and get where they ultimately want to go.

Mike, you said half of your personal clients are business owners. Did that happen organically?

Mike Proctor: Well, being the Founder, I've always had an entrepreneurial spark. So I think I resonate really well with other like-minded folks. And, naturally, that has led to my client base. But one thing that always perplexed me when I got into this business was being under the impression that all financial advisors are money guys and business savvy. It just isn't the case. In fact, most of our industry isn't really wired to service business owners. And so I was a little bit disappointed with my finance background. After several years of working in the industry, I just decided, "Hey, I can do this in a different way that would help a huge, underserved segment of entrepreneurs, while at the same time serving others in a way that doesn't have the product agenda with incentivized bonuses for hitting certain targets." I wanted to serve with a focus on the client's individual needs.

What are some unique challenges that business owners face?

Mike Proctor: There is one fundamental challenge, and that's getting out of your own way. As a business owner, I've got more of a mind that looks at strategy and vision and asks, "Where can we take this? How can we get there in the most efficient way possible?" But my biggest weak spots are marketing and salesmanship. When someone has a passion for going out and starting a company, they know what they know *really* well. But they also have blind spots. And our blind spot was definitely marketing. We've come to find that it was actually a unique competitive advantage for us if we could harness it. And so, over the last year and a half, we've been on a journey of figuring that out. We have a long way to go. But I guess just from personal experience, you don't know what you don't know and sometimes in a huge way, and it speaks to how important it is to get the right people on the bus and lean into the team on engaging the areas that you're not the strongest in. Don't be afraid to hand off those hats and get out of the way of the team.

Has the recent pandemic caused changes in the financial services field?

Mike Proctor: I think it has been a wake-up call for some when it comes to their next steps, whether it be transitioning their business to the next leaders or selling it, retiring, and giving themselves the flexibility to focus on what matters most to them. The pandemic has been stressful for business owners and everyday families in many different ways, aside from just health. The pandemic provided an excellent checkpoint for people to focus on what comes next. If their identity was wrapped up in their business, and they saw the business being put at risk, they might have to reconcile and figure that out. Many business owners might think, "Hey, maybe this isn't the best place to be centered." And now they are starting to look outside of that.

Are there common mistakes you help business owners avoid?

Mike Proctor: Absolutely. One of the biggest mistakes is leaving succession planning for when a business owner is ready to retire or transition the business. Succession planning should begin when you start the business because once that thing is going and you pass away unexpectedly, it is a total mess for your clients. In addition, other employees in the company might have to spend some time in court to sort it all out. So you've got to start before you're ready to sell. Frankly, the best time to be able to sell is when you have a willing buyer. And just because you're ready to sell at some point doesn't mean that a willing buyer will show up either. It typically takes about five years to get a business ready to transition. And even though you may not be wanting to sell or be ready to sell, it needs to be prepared to transition because there are so many other life events that can pop up that may force that to happen anyways.

What are the advantages of early planning?

Mike Proctor: Starting early in planning the transition gives your employees and clients peace of mind. It also helps the owner sleep better at night, knowing they will not leave a legacy that is a huge mess. Nobody wants to be remembered for all the cleanup that had to be done after they were gone. And I think it's really an act of love to your family and those that work with you and for you if your business can transition in a healthy way.

Mike, what inspired you to get started in the financial services industry?

Mike Proctor: Back in college, I was a member of an organization called the Navigators. And one of the concepts that impressed me was if you want to know what is important to someone, look at their calendar and checkbook to see where their time and money go. I didn't see a big career opportunity in scheduling people's calendars. But from a young age, I loved starting businesses, haggling, making deals, and earning money my own way. So it was natural for me to want to help families, couples, and business owners with their finances and goals to make that substantial bottom-line impact. I also saw it as an avenue to have the level of conversations that would promote more leadership within the family unit and at home. Let's face it, money is such a touchy area to discuss and the level of trusting relationships that can be built in this space allows for deeply meaningful and impactful conversations in other areas over time. It has been very special for me to be part of that for our clients as I witness transformation, steps of faith, and earnest steps seeking to serve the other spouse.

What advice do you have for people trying to choose a financial advisor?

Mike Proctor: Shared beliefs are very important for an advisor to encourage you down the path you want to go. For example, if a client has a strong faith, it will be very connected to what they do with their money. So looking for an advisor with similar beliefs and values is critical.

Also, ask how they are paid and make sure you are very clear on that. Are there bonuses and incentives? Do they get paid more for selling in-house products? Consider the scope of work because it is really easy for an advisor to do the commoditized aspect of the industry, which is just managing a portfolio. We do that for hundreds of clients. And if we just stop there, our job is simple. It does add value, but maybe not as much as when you get down to what really matters most for a client. Clients need to understand how much interaction they will get with their advisor to move the needle and enjoy their life.

How can people find you, connect with you, and learn more?

Mike Proctor: Our website is www.leadingedgefp.com. You can call our office to schedule an appointment with me or another advisor at 316-768-7526.

MIKE PROCTOR, CFP®, RICP®, CVGA

Founding President

Leading Edge Financial Planning, LLC

Mike is a CERTIFIED FINANCIAL PLANNER® with more than ten years of industry experience and founded Leading Edge Financial Planning, LLC in 2017 as an RIA in Kansas. He saw an opportunity to grow a firm that can change the focus of the financial planning industry and how clients are engaged at a deeper level to help clients make wise financial decisions. Mike also founded Leading Edge Growth, LLC to help his entrepreneur clients with strategic growth rooted in a proprietary valuation process that scores core business functions and identifies opportunities in their company-specific risk to help them leverage the strategic planning process. He truly cares about the impact within the family around leadership and money matters, tells groan-worthy dad jokes to his three kids, and loves cheering on the K-State Wildcats. Mike is located at the Wichita office, has served on Goddard City Council since 2020, is a Boardmember of Wichita Estate Planning Council, is active in his church community, and has his finance degree from Kansas State University.

WEBSITE: www.leadingedgefp.com

PHONE: 316-768-7526

CHRISTIEN HUGHES

CHRISTIEN HUGHES

Conversation with Christien Hughes

Christien, you are a Financial Advisor out of Scottsdale, Arizona, with First Command Financial Services. Tell us about your work and the people you help.

Christien Hughes: I'm retired military, and our company works with veterans and young military people who don't necessarily have a lot of capital coming in to invest. But they want to start even if they don't have a lot to invest. We don't chase wealth; we build wealth. I specialize in working with retirees, as there are not many military families here in Scottsdale. In addition, I focus on educating the youth about how to invest for long-term financial success.

How has the pandemic impacted the financial services industry?

Christien Hughes: The pandemic highlighted the need to have savings, investments, and insurance. People now have a sense of urgency about their financial planning and realize they can't afford to wait around.

What are the most common questions or concerns your clients have?

Christien Hughes: "Will I have enough to retire?" I hear this question a lot. It used to be that if you worked hard, you would automatically have enough to retire. But now, people are doubting social security and genuinely concerned about their ability to retire. Another one is, "Will I leave a legacy?" People want to leave something for their family members and children.

Are there any myths or misconceptions that prevent people from getting their finances in order?

Christien Hughes: People think you need to have a lot of money to invest. But you can start with just $100 a month and build from there. It can be a difficult adjustment for people to put money away and not see or touch it. So people fear it. But long-term growth is like planting a seed. You don't necessarily know when that seed will sprout, but you can't dig up the seed because it may very well be about to shoot through the soil.

How can people be assured their money is not at risk when working with a Financial Advisor?

Christien Hughes: I use the analogy of a rollercoaster. If you are in the market, it's a rollercoaster ride. If you are young, you can afford a little more risk, and you are probably sitting in the front seat of the coaster. As you age, you may want to move closer to the back. There are some things at the back of the rollercoaster, such as annuities that have protections so that if there is a downturn in the market, you can avoid substantial losses. Bonds are also considered more conservative investments because they are not based on the stock market's volatility.

Are there common mistakes that you help people avoid?

Christien Hughes: People often don't understand how detrimental high-interest rates can be to your financial success. If you have $1,000 debt and pay $200 in interest a month, it takes $200 away from what you could be saving. I like to see people switching their mindset to, "I can invest, and I don't need to have credit."

Christien, what inspired you to get started in the financial services industry?

Christien Hughes: This is my purpose. I am a man of faith. When I was getting ready to retire from the Air Force, my Financial Advisor asked me if I had ever thought about doing this. At the time, I said, "No." But I had a conversation with God. And I said, "Okay, God, what am I going to be when I grow up?" He said, "Well, I gave you a purpose." I have three personal cornerstones: Faith, Family, and Finances. And I received these in 2008. By 2015 when I was ready to retire, God let me know that these cornerstones made up my purpose. When you know your purpose, you find joy in fulfilling it.

What are the most important things to consider when choosing a Financial Advisor?

Christien Hughes: There is not one aspect of your life that finances don't touch. So having a personal relationship with your advisor is key. You should feel comfortable with this person and have meaningful conversations. We all have similar products. But you need to trust the person you are giving your money to.

How can people find you, connect with you, and learn more?

Christien Hughes: You can find me on Facebook through my name, as well as LinkedIn. My email is cnhuges@firstcommand.com, or you can reach me by phone at 480-386-7005.

CHRISTIEN HUGHES

Financial Advisor

First Command Financial Services

Christien Hughes is a Financial Advisor with First Command Financial Services, Inc and is based in Scottsdale, Arizona. He is a United States Air Force veteran, retiring as a Major. After his time in the military, he was called to be of service in a different capacity as a financial advisor and has been working in financial services for five years. He has a Bachelor of Science from LSU and a Master of Science from Trident University International.

Chris' personal cornerstones are Faith, Family, and Finance. He believes that his purpose is to be an inspiration and a source of knowledge and wisdom to his clients and anyone who seeks growth in these three areas. His goal is to help 1000 families in their pursuit of financial security.

LEADING ADVISOR

Chris was born in Chicago, IL, but moved to rural Mississippi as a teenager. During his military career, his travels took him to all corners of the United States. Additionally, he has lived in Saudi Arabia, Bahrain, Israel and traveled to many other countries. He believes that his broad background enables him to connect with his clients on many different levels to earn the trust necessary to be a good financial advisor.

Outside of work, Chris enjoys spending time with his two teenage sons and investing in their growth as young men. His mentorship does not stop at his family; he is also very active in Men's ministry. His openness about his own journey enables him to encourage and teach in a way that doesn't make learning a chore. He is quick to remind everyone that being from the south taught him how to make a short story long, but he takes pride in knowing that his anecdotes and analogies are funny and educational at the same time.

EMAIL: cnhughes@firstcommand.com

PHONE: 480-386-7005

ABBY SANTIAGO

ABBY SANTIAGO, CFP®, CLU®

Conversation with Abby Santiago, CFP®, CLU®

Abby, you are the Co-Founder of the Florida Wealth Planning Group. Tell us about your work and the people you help.

Abby Santiago: Florida Wealth Planning Group was established in 2007. My partner and I went from being individual advisors to creating a joint practice. We are now 20 advisors in 9 locations across Florida. It's quite exciting to see that we are uniting with advisors who got pushed out from some of the bigger outfits because they weren't producing large numbers. They have a client-centric focus instead of numbers, so those are the advisors who join us and do a wonderful job serving our clients, ranging from young professionals to entrepreneurs. And then, of course, we are here in Florida, where there are several retirees, so we help with retirement income tax planning and estate planning.

How has the pandemic impacted the financial services industry?

Abby Santiago: You know, it's really interesting because no one could have predicted this pandemic. And certainly, no one could have predicted that the dip of 37% we saw in March of 2020 would recover as quickly as it has. We had a record year in 2020. And thus far, 2021 has been a strong year. We have discovered a couple of things.

First of all, we were really prepared to do virtual meetings. And so, we are still doing virtual meetings, which has freed up a lot of time since we are not traveling to several different cities that we work in. The other thing, from a client-centric point of view, is the pandemic helped our clients to start examining their values. Where do they want to spend their time, energy, and resources? We often take our family and relationships for granted. And this pandemic has helped us come back and look at what's truly important. And it's interesting because we've done some longevity seminars and learned that scientifically, your social interactions are the most significant predictors of longevity and good health, even above genetics, exercise, and diet. I think it's been easy for all of us to grasp that concept during this pandemic.

Did the pandemic change people's mindsets about getting their financial affairs in order?

Abby Santiago: When you have nothing else to do, you start cleaning your own house. Finances certainly cause people stress. So if you can get your finances under control, or at least create a plan that will get you back in control, you will naturally see the stress level start to drop. And just like the people who finally found time to go to Home Depot to fix that leaky sink that has been dripping for years, people started coming through our doors to talk about their financial plans.

The other surprising thing was that I had recent college graduates reach out to me to learn financial literacy and not just all the hype about Bitcoin and day trading. They wanted to understand tax codes, what types of accounts they should open, whether they should have traditional or Roth IRAs, and how much they should put in their pre-tax 401Ks. So I now teach a class every Wednesday night and find myself having fascinating conversations with 22 and 23-year-olds. At that age, I wasn't even thinking about finances.

When is the right time to start financial planning?

Abby Santiago: I always say there's a formula; it's time and money. If you don't have a lot of one, you'll need a lot of the other. So the sooner you start, the better. I love talking to 17, 18, and 19-year-olds because saving is a habit, just like studying and exercising. The number one mistake I see is that people wait until they have a big chunk of money to start investing. The smartest and most successful way to really create wealth is to start saving at whatever level you can. It doesn't matter if it's $10 a week or $10 a month. And then you just continue to up the ante. Whenever you're not feeling like you are drowning, you can raise the dollar amount a little bit. And you will create good habits. I have clients in their 80s that have established excellent saving habits, and if they don't save, they feel like something is very wrong. It's just in their ingrained genetics; it is part of who they are, to save more than they spend. I would phrase it as "living below your means."

Are there any myths or misconceptions that prevent people from starting their financial plans?

Abby Santiago: A lot of people think it's expensive. Florida Wealth Planning Group, which is Ameriprise as a whole, has a foundational plan that we start with at no charge. It's a great way to begin the process. As you elevate and get more complicated, your advisor will talk to you about the different ways to work with them on a fee-base, commission-base, or some combination of both. It's only expensive if you take action, and it turns out to be the wrong action for getting you to where you want to go.

Abby, what inspired you to get started in the financial services industry?

Abby Santiago: I grew up Latina with a grandmother in my home, and she preached to save for a rainy day, a penny saved is $1 earned; all that stuff. She was born in the 1920s. And as a young person, of course, I did whatever a young person does, and it went in one ear and out the other.

I happened to be running a chain of restaurants out in California at the time. I was very successful, lived in Malibu overlooking the Pacific Ocean, drove a sports car, and had *nothing* saved. I did a smart thing and invested in a piece of real estate, intending to have a tenant in Culver City. So I closed on the property, and the next day I got a court notice saying I had to let the current tenant live there for six months for free or pay her $5,000 to move out. And then I went to work, and I got laid off. So all of a sudden, I realized, "Holy moly, everything Grandma told me was correct."

I started to explore where I wanted to go from there. I was a math major. I loved math, and because of my experience in the restaurant industry, I knew that I really enjoyed people. What could I do to combine these two? California had financed a program for recently laid-off individuals to train as stockbroker sales assistants, and I got my first job at Lehman Brothers. That's how I got my foot in the door.

What should people look for when choosing a Financial Advisor?

Abby Santiago: The key to working with an advisor is to pick someone you can relate to. I always tell my partner, "If people talk to you about their money, they will talk to you about anything. They will tell you things they don't even tell their best friend." So pick someone you feel comfortable with. That is the number one component of a successful advisor relationship.

How can people find you, connect with you, and learn more?

Abby Santiago: Our website is www.ameripriseadvisors.com/team/florida-wealth-planning-group/. You can also reach me via telephone at 386-597-2994 or email at abigail.x.santiago@ampf.com.

ABBY SANTIAGO, CFP®, CLU®

Co-Founder

Florida Wealth Planning Group

My name is Abigail Santiago. For over 30 years, I have been a Certified Financial Planner and Chartered Life Underwriter whose main goal was to cause action in areas where there has not been enough money management. I am also the Co-Founder and Managing Partner of Florida Wealth Planning Group, a private wealth advisory practice of Ameriprise Financial Services, LLC. My mission as a professional in finance is to empower clients to achieve financial freedom so that they give their time, talents, and resources to the things that matter most.

Aside from being a financial advisor, I am an avid gardener and love to destress through nature. From 2010 to 2014, I was given the opportunity to host, produce, and direct a radio show known as "Healthy, Wealthy & Wise with Abby." In this broadcast, I answered questions and talked about issues relating to personal finances, well-being, and happiness. On top of that, I was blessed with two sons, twin daughters, and I am a happy grandparent to two boys. While parenting, I became proficient in communication, managing expectations, and above all, the creation of possibilities.

ADDRESS: Ameriprise Financial Services, LLC
10 Florida Park Drive North
Suite D
Palm Coast, FL 32137

WEBSITE: www.ameripriseadvisors.com/team/florida-wealth-planning-group/

EMAIL: abigail.x.santiago@ampf.com

PHONE: 386-597-2994

FAX: 386-597-2997

LM "STAMP" STAMPER

LM "STAMP" STAMPER

Conversation with LM "Stamp" Stamper

LM, you are the Founder of LMStamper.com. You are affectionately known as "Stamp." Tell us about your work and the people you help.

LM Stamper: I am a Financial Planner in the Dallas, Fort Worth area going on almost 11 years now. I am an RICP® - which is a Retirement Income Certified Professional, and my primary clients are retirees, soon-to-be retirees, and female professionals. I take a holistic approach as it relates to financial planning. So we don't just look at investments; we look at the entire picture, such as income in retirement, taxes, Medicare, and even estate planning.

What drove you to work with those particular types of clients?

LM Stamper: When I first started in the field, I worked with dentists. But as time went on, I gravitated toward working with female professionals as I found it to be an underserved demographic. Statistics show that women own over 50% of the wealth in this country. And when you're working with married retirees, statistically, the male passes before the female. So as a financial advisor working with people who are over the 60-year-old mark, later in life, we end up continuing our working relationship with the surviving spouse, who is often the woman. Not to mention, I have a three-year-old daughter who I want to be financially savvy, and I would like to see more financial education provided to the female population in general.

How has the recent pandemic affected the financial services industry?

LM Stamper: You would have thought 2020 would be a down year for financial planning, but the opposite happened. Of course, we had clients who needed to access accounts because of financial hardships and job loss, but we also had clients who simply realized they needed to pay more attention to their finances. The pandemic opened people's eyes to the importance of liquidity and making sure they could not only access funds without penalty but that it would be enough to carry them through the storm. Many people needed access to 6 months or a year's worth of living expenses, and thankfully we do the type of planning that prepares people for that type of situation.

Are there common myths or misconceptions that prevent people from getting their finances in order?

LM Stamper: People think that working with a Financial Advisor will involve high costs. That's just not the case. Different planners have different fee structures, so a planner can meet your needs no matter where you are in life financially. Sometimes people get a little bit intimidated. If you turn on the stock channel, you see all these graphs and big words being used. I like to keep it simple. At the end of the day, just save a percentage of your income, do it consistently, diversify where you are putting it, and protect yourself from life's biggest threats. Do that, and you will be just fine.

What is the biggest fear that retirees have, and how do you help them with that challenge?

LM Stamper: Well, as you can imagine, there are a number of fears when you step off into retirement, such as rising healthcare costs, taxes, a down stock market, etc. But I would say the fear of outliving one's money consistently rises to the top. Luckily, we specialize in retirement income planning, so this is one of the issues that we tackle right out of the gate. We do that by making sure that no matter what, they have income that they can never outlive, as well as a sufficient bucket of money to access when life decides to "change its mind." If this is a fear that people have; I always encourage them to reach out to me, and I'd be more than happy to answer any questions they have and show them how we alleviate that risk.

You mentioned that advisors have different wealth structures. Can you talk about what these are?

LM Stamper: Some advisors will just charge a fee for service, which is kind of like going to a CPA or an attorney. They sit down and say, "Hey, I'll outline what you should do. And I'll just charge you a flat, one-time fee." Secondarily, and probably the most common structure, is assets under management. As the advisor manages those assets and moves them from here to there, they charge a management fee. And lastly, sometimes advisors are paid by the vendors they work with. So in certain financial planning scenarios, you're going to purchase a product, and when doing so, the company you choose will pay the advisor out of the company's pocket.

Personally, I'm not a big fee-for-service guy. I always tell folks that I cringe at the thought of you writing out a check to me personally. I never want that. But it comes down to whatever works for you. Some people say, "Hey, I don't want a long-term relationship. I just need a quick fix. So tell me what to do. And I'll take that information and be on my way." And that's fine, too, if that works for your situation.

When is the right time to start planning?

LM Stamper: I like to joke and say, especially us guys, that we don't get serious about our money until around age 30. Most of the time, people just aren't paying attention when they're young. But I do have clients who start out in their mid-20s right out of college, which is really smart. If you haven't done much planning, you will definitely feel a sense of urgency once you reach the age of 55 since retirement is right around the corner. But I tell people all the time, don't hesitate to reach out to me, regardless of where you are in life. It's never too late to start.

Stamp, what inspired you to get started in the financial services industry?

LM Stamper: Well, I've always loved business and numbers. I actually have a real estate background. I affectionately and comedically say, "I was recruited away and duped into this business over ten years ago," but it's the best thing that ever happened to me. And I love teaching. Whenever there is a subject I feel I am well versed in, I enjoy sharing that knowledge with other people. All of those characteristics drew me to the financial services industry.

What is important to consider when choosing a Financial Advisor?

LM Stamper: Many advisors do more talking than listening. It's essential to find someone who listens to you and is interested in what keeps you up at night. This will more than likely be a long-term relationship, so certainly find someone who you feel comfortable with and can trust. Lastly, your advisor should give you an opportunity to learn. Some clients like to get into the nuts and bolts, while others like to keep it high-level. Either way, education should be part of the process. And, most importantly, have fun! Work with someone who isn't a "fuddy-duddy." Finances don't always have to be so serious.

How do people find you, connect with you, and learn more?

LM Stamper: The easiest way is to Google "LM Stamper," which will pull up my website, client reviews, Facebook, and LinkedIn accounts. My website is www.LMStamper.com. Also, feel free to call or text at 817-846-3005, and if you'd like to hop on my calendar for a quick chat, you can always go to www.TalkToStamp.com.

LM "STAMP" STAMPER

Managing Director

www.LMStamper.com

LM Stamper's ("Stamp") mission is to help educate women about the laws of money so that they can make better, more informed decisions regarding their finances and enjoy a comfortable and fulfilling retirement.

Stamp has been a retirement advisor for over ten years and has won various awards for accomplishments in the education and implementation of financial strategies for his clients, as well as for the development of new advisors.

LEADING ADVISOR

Using a powerful model that begins with education first, Stamp helps his clients move toward a position of financial independence in their lives. His value to the public lies in his desire to educate his clients first and to help provide them with the appropriate financial tools they need to achieve proper financial balance and enjoy a thriving retirement.

Stamp grew up as an Army brat, traveling the world with his family from Los Angeles, Lubbock, Austin, and Germany. He's thankful to have seen what the world has to offer and now proudly makes Texas his home with his beautiful wife and daughter.

In his spare time, Stamp can be found painting, enjoying good movies, cooking, listening to music, watching sports, and mentoring his Little Brother via the Big Brothers Big Sisters program. Still, his favorite activity outside of the office is fantasy football. He's the commissioner of his league with good friends of over 24 years, and he says it never seems to get old.

WEBSITE: www.LMStamper.com

PHONE: 817-846-3005

TONY DE SANTIS

TONY DE SANTIS

Conversation with Tony De Santis

Tony, you are a Wealth Advisor and the Founder of The Direct Effect. Tell us about your work and the people you help.

Tony De Santis: We are a full-scale financial planning firm. Our goal is to help anybody who is beginning to wonder, "Do I have enough money set aside for retirement? Is that money going to last? Is it set up correctly?" Unfortunately, we have found that most people do not know the answers to those questions, even if they are working with someone. So we help our clients through a very holistic approach and work to create a complete plan for their retirement.

Is there a common question people have about finances?

Tony De Santis: Over the last couple of months, the most common question I get is, "What about taxes?" Most people these days have the bulk of their retirement savings in IRAs, 401Ks, or 403Bs. A common fear is that since they didn't pay taxes on that money in the past, they will lose a large portion of their retirement savings if taxes start going up in the future.

There are six different ways people can grow money completely tax-free. We help our clients work through each of those six ways to minimize the Internal Revenue Service's lien on their retirement accounts. In addition, we also analyze how their current assets are invested. Of the assets they have, how much is tax-deferred? How much is tax-free? How much is non-taxable? We then help them rotate those numbers around to find an optimal balance for their portfolio.

Are there any myths or misconceptions people have about financial planning?

Tony De Santis: Unfortunately, the biggest misconception that most people have is if the market goes down, it will come back. Many clients believe that if they just hold on long enough, they'll be alright. But if you are in the retirement red zone, either the last five years before you retire or the first five years after you retire, it can be dangerous. If the market takes a hit during that time, you may not have enough cash or time for the money to grow back.

What types of things should people do in the "retirement red zone?"

Tony De Santis: Make sure that a certain percentage of your assets are protected, meaning they will not go down when the stock market goes down. Many people believe they are diversified because they own many different mutual funds or exchange-traded funds. But when we do the analysis and run those funds through the computer, we're able to see that a lot of those mutual funds and exchange-traded funds hold the exact same stocks as the other ones that they have. So if the market goes down, everything they have is going down with it. We need to ensure that our clients have protection through certain assets that will not be affected by the stock market.

What mistakes do you help your clients avoid?

Tony De Santis: People's biggest mistake is not starting to save early enough. If we had all started saving in our 20s, we would be in much better shape. We don't have time machines, so we can't go back and change the past. The second mistake is not making a change TODAY. I named my company The

Direct Effect because I have always believed the decisions you make and actions you take TODAY will directly affect your retirement. I always tell potential clients to take action today, whether they choose to work with me or someone else. The time you have between now and when you retire gets shorter and shorter, and the quicker you take action, the more options you have before that time comes.

Do you need a lot of money to get started?

Tony De Santis: I spoke with a young woman yesterday. And she said, "Tony, I just don't have a whole lot of money in my budget." And I said, "Could you find $10 a week, maybe $40 or $50 a month?" She said, "I think I can do that." So we started there. Doing something effective with $50 a month begins to build the habit. Once you start seeing that growth, the benefits become very tangible. And then you can increase the amount slowly from there.

Tony, what inspired you to get started in the financial services field?

Tony De Santis: I graduated from UCLA in 1992 and started in financial services at that point. I realized that most people have no idea how the stock market and finances really work. I love educating people and showing them how all of these things work together. In the 30 years since then, our world has become so much more complex. In our parents' or grandparents' time, they started at a company, worked there for their entire career, got a pension, got social security, and it replaced their income. It doesn't work like that anymore. And now all these different cogs in the machine have to work together. And that's why I always use this word, and I use it way too much. We have to look at a *holistic* plan for each client. And when I see that plan and all the little pieces coming together, it fills me with a sense of accomplishment. I love being able to do that for my clients.

What should people look for when choosing an advisor?

Tony De Santis: Number one, make sure your advisor is independent. There are too many advisors who can only represent one company or one particular set of products or portfolios. Number two, make sure the advisor is a fiduciary. There are plenty of advisors out there who do not act in a fiduciary capacity. And they're not looking out for the client's best interests. Number three, you should absolutely find somebody who will look at an entire holistic plan. Many advisors only concentrate on one element: insurance, investments, or estate planning. My hope is that everybody finds an advisor who can handle all of those things together.

How can people find you, connect with you, and learn more?

Tony De Santis: My website is www.thedirecteffect.com. You can also call me directly at 303-717-4721. I'm always available to help people out.

TONY DE SANTIS

Wealth Advisor and Founder

The Direct Effect

Tony De Santis has taught more than 10,000 people about how to create a worry-free retirement by generating an ongoing retirement income. Tony places a key emphasis on both income generation (in any type of market environment) as well as capital preservation. Tony has over twenty-five years of experience in the financial arena. He is passionate about empowering individuals, couples, and business owners with knowledge regarding taking control of their financial futures. He earned his Bachelor of Arts degree in Economics from the University of California, Los Angeles, and he now lives and works in Denver, Colorado

– although he is able to work virtually with clients throughout the United States. When not working, Tony enjoys restoring classic cars and spending time with his wife and four rescue dogs.

WEBSITE: www.thedirecteffect.com

PHONE: 303-717-4721

JOHN NOWICKI

JOHN NOWICKI

Conversation with John Nowicki

John, you are a Co-Founder of LCM Capital Management. Tell us about your work and the people you help.

John Nowicki: My partner and I started the firm 22 years ago. We have both been in the business for over 34 years. We started LCM Capital Management as an investment advisor because much of what we observed on the retail side was about the firm making money rather than what was in the client's interests. LCM stands for "low-cost management." Our belief is really simple. People are often overcharged to have their money managed. We want to educate the clients on the costs, buried fees, and risks involved and simplify the business. Our services can positively impact everyone, but our typical client falls in the $10 million and below range. Over the years, we've seen many clients with two or three different investment relationships and some money spread out who think they're diversified. But when we sit down with them to show them exactly what they own, it turns out they are invested in all the same things, just wearing different suits. This is a prime example of how we educate people and show them what happens below the surface.

What are some common challenges your clients face?

John Nowicki: Under-diversification, over-paying in fees, and not having enough income in retirement pose the three biggest challenges for any investor. Investors tend to chase performance and what has worked in the past but may not work in the future. My industry just loves to create investment products out of investment ideas that are presently working and push the money flow into those. Well, far too often, whatever was working doesn't work anymore. So our philosophy embraces staying diversified and staying the course. Don't just chase whatever seems to be the hot subject or asset class of the day.

How has the recent pandemic impacted the financial services industry?

John Nowicki: It's a dose of reality. From our perspective, we manage our client's money with low turnover and do not try to time the market. I think back to March of 2020 when the world was ending. Everyone was staying indoors and washing their vegetables. I mean, it was bad. But we put out a piece talking about staying the course and staying invested in the stock market. We believe if you don't try to time it, the results can be dramatically better. It's a cliche, but it's true - it's time in the market, not timing the market that matters. My numbers will be off slightly, but relatively speaking, if you missed the best 20 trading days from 2000 to 2019, your rate of return went from just over 6% to almost nothing. Which is crazy, right? That's 20 trading days out of roughly 4800 trading days, which is less than one-half of 1% of those days, The point being nobody, and I mean nobody, can predict which 20 trading days out of more than 4800, those will be.

The pandemic also made people realize they need cash on hand for a rainy day. Cash doesn't make a lot of money today. But cash comes in very handy when you are scared and hunkered down. Again, having that diversification helps to take the edge off. Most people we talk to have no idea what they spend monthly, no matter where they fall when it comes to wealth. The pandemic increased awareness of spending. What are we really spending money on? People find out they spend way more money than they thought on things they don't even need. And that money can be put away to reach the goal of a more comfortable retirement.

Are there myths and misconceptions that prevent people from planning?

John Nowicki: People think they don't have enough money to start investing. Our industry focuses on wealthy people. But it's all relative, right? $10,000 may be a lot of money to one person and a drop in the bucket to another. That's where our business fits in. We don't really have a minimum investment. You don't need a lot of money to be diversified. We use ETFs (exchange-traded index funds) as part of our portfolio allocation to give clients instant diversification. The reality is, you don't have to have a lot of money to invest and to have someone help you do it properly.

What mistakes do you help people avoid?

John Nowicki: We never want people to spend an excessive amount of money to have their money managed. And often, people are spending way more than they ever imagined. We sit down with our clients and show them the all-in costs of their investments. "Hey, here's what you're paying for X, here's what you're paying for Y, let's put this all together." And then a light goes on for them.

We believe what we do is unique. Most people don't realize how much they are paying in fees or how much risk they are taking with their investments. They often don't know that there is a better way. Sometimes it can be difficult to help people understand why their financial future is at risk and why they need to act. The most fulfilling part of my job is when a prospective client realizes what is possible for their money.

Again, under-diversification is another big mistake we help people remedy. We don't own mutual funds; we hate them. We refer to them as the great American rip-off. They were created to make money for the house, right? There has always been a joke that if you want to make a lot of money in our industry, start a mutual fund. They focus on particular areas and sectors, and the money flows into these things, leaving the clients very little control. We explain to prospective clients that three things affect every investment in the world: fees, taxes, and inflation. The only one that is uncontrollable is inflation. Fees, you always have to pay them. If anyone ever tells you it's free, run. Once again, you have to pay taxes, but if you can control them, reduce them and/or defer them, you will be way ahead of the game. The problem with mutual funds is that you don't have control of either the taxable distributions or the fees.

The third mistake we help clients avoid is not having enough income to sustain their retirement.

Most investors focus on the growth of their portfolio but do not consider the income that it generates. We review income and expenses with all of our clients so they understand exactly what comes in, what goes out, and when their money will run out. One major expense that most clients do not account for is healthcare costs. The average couple retiring in 2021 can expect to spend approximately $300,000 for medical expenses throughout retirement. We make sure clients think about the types of events that can derail their retirement, both expected and unexpected.

As a result, LCM Capital Management focuses on; reducing client fees, controlling and reducing their taxes, and optimizing their portfolio income. So we explain these types of things to prospective clients. Honestly, it's a very simple business. But my industry makes it more complicated and then charges more money for that complexity. It doesn't need to be that way.

John, how did you get started in the financial services field?

John Nowicki: I started in September of 1987, right before the crash. So that was my wake-up call. I like to tell people I didn't have any clients invested in the stock market crash of '87, which is a true statement because I didn't have any clients! When my partner and I started this business, I had four kids and a second mortgage. My wife wasn't working, and I ended up going to the bank for a third mortgage. And the banker said, "You know, Johnny, there's nothing here." So that was when I realized that I needed to get my arms around my finances and cost of living. I am a living, breathing example of a person who didn't come from the "right" side of the tracks.

My father worked three jobs and raised seven children along with my mother. So when I meet my clients, I can relate to all of that.

When my children graduated from college, I sat down with them and said, "Congratulations, your graduation gift is I'm going to take on your student debt so you can start life debt-free. Now let's talk about 401ks and investing." This is when my wife tells me, "you're scaring the kids," and my answer to her is, "no, I'm preparing our kids." You tell a 23-year-old they have to start putting $700 a month away (I explain to them they need to take the amount of what their student loan payment would have been and double it), and as you can imagine, they look at you like you are crazy. That's a lot of money for them! But I tell them to put $700 a month away and add your company's 401k match. Now run it at a 5% rate of return over the next 30 years, then come and tell me what you think. By the age of 55, they will probably have more money than I ever had in my entire life! They are now hooked, and that's the greatest gift I can give my kids besides the example of my wonderful, loving marriage.

So that is why I do what I do. I am passionate about educating people to prepare for retirement. Statistics show that about 40% of Americans ages 60 and older rely on Social Security as their sole income during retirement. But the frightening thing is, the average Social Security benefit as of 2020 is only $1,503 a month or $18,036 a year. I don't know very many people who can survive on that. It's nice to see the light go on for people when you explain this. When it comes to planning, the earlier, the better. You have time on your side, but it's never too late to start.

What should people look for when choosing an advisor?

John Nowicki: Make sure they are a fiduciary. That word is starting to pick up some steam in the industry. It means we are legally obligated to put our client's interests first. Ask the advisor for their ADV and CRS documents to verify they are a fiduciary. Once that box is checked, you know there is an obligation for you to come first.

Find out what the costs are to have your money managed. Not just their fee, but any fees that are a part of the investments they recommend. Is the advisor obligated to use particular families of funds or products? Can you use any investment that exists, or are you beholden to a specific set? These details can definitely have an impact on your long-term investing success.

How can people find you, connect with you, and learn more?

John Nowicki: Our website is www.lcmcapital.com, and my email address is jnowicki@lcmcapital.com. If you would prefer to call, our number is 312-705-3013. We don't charge to sit down and talk with you. As we often tell people, you may not like the answers we give you, but they will be honest answers. Ultimately, we want you to be educated because the topic is so important.

JOHN NOWICKI

Co-Founder, President, and CCO

LCM Capital Management

John Nowicki is the co-founder, President, and CCO of LCM Capital Management. He has over 33 years of industry experience. He spends his days helping executives, physicians, and business owners prepare for their retirement dreams by reducing costs, taxes and balancing risk.

During John's 15 years in various roles with multiple companies, he saw firsthand how the industry worked, and he did not like it. Early in his career, he saw firms encouraging sales of particular funds or managers for his clients in cases that might have been good for the firm but not necessarily what was best for the client.

As a result, too many people were losing money through high or buried fees and uncontrolled taxes and risk. He thought the only way to right this wrong was to start his own firm, which he did 20 years ago with his partner, Gary Wozny. John developed a strong passion for educating his clients on their fees, taxes, and risks by providing a transparent financial alternative and approach to investing. He believes this approach has brought positive change into his clients' lives and is often the very reason his clients regularly refer their friends, family members, and associates to him.

John has a bachelor's degree in financial management from Indiana University Bloomington. When he's not working, John enjoys spending time with Maria, his wife of 32 years, and their four adult children. John loves to take family vacations, including his favorite hobbies of golfing, fishing, and boring his children on the importance of planning for their retirement. John has taught 5th-grade religious education at his local parochial school for the past six years. He has been an usher at Sunday mass for the last 25 years and has held several positions within the parish, including being a founding member of the Parish Finance Council.

WEBSITE: www.LCMcapital.com

EMAIL: LCM@LCMcapital.com

PHONE: 312-705-3013

KEVEN PRATHER

KEVEN PRATHER, CFBS

Conversation with Keven Prather, CFBS

Keven, you are the Founder of TransitioNext Advisors. Tell us about your work and the people you help.

Keven Prather: We do personalized total wealth planning for individuals who own businesses. The goal is to integrate their business with their personal wealth strategy, often to prepare for an exit or a transition to ownership in a key employee group, trust, ESOP, or generational family members taking over the business. In that effort, we handle complicated insurance placements and create frameworks for our client's investments that allow them to live lives of significance on their terms.

What unique challenges do business owners face?

Keven Prather: As you know, Congress is contemplating some major tax changes. We see a tremendous amount of activity in mergers and acquisitions. Business owners want to sell their businesses because they are worried about an uncertain future tax landscape. They want to secure what they know now. So uncertainty is a significant concern. The baby boomer generation is defining what is happening currently in our economy. As the baby boomers exit and transition their companies, it affects everyone. Frankly, it creates a massive amount of opportunity for younger people to take over those companies. Supply chain issues, labor shortages, and trade labor all impact business owners as well. Much change is happening, and the pace of change seems to be accelerating.

Are there common myths and misconceptions that you hear from your clients?

Keven Prather: They think the government will confiscate their money with proposed changes in the banking regulations, which further extends the Anti-Money Laundering Act. I just had a conversation with a client yesterday, and I had to calm him down a bit. I let him know that they would not take his money and that more reporting requirements were coming out. He wondered if he should pull all of his money out of the banks. And though this is an extreme example, I also find it to be a current example.

There is a lot of misinformation out there. As soon as Congress can settle in on the tax policies for the next few years, things will calm down a little bit. There is an awful lot of discussion about the labor shortage and what is causing that. The pandemic has a lot to do with it, as businesses have to get ahead of the curve and adjust to a new normal. To a large extent, their labor forces may not want to work inside the buildings, especially in the higher-tech or B2B businesses that can have work completed from remote offices. In manufacturing, it's a little more challenging because you have to be where the machinery is to make things. In certain direct service-based businesses like medicine, it's more complicated because you have to be where your equipment is and where the patients are. But employers have to be a lot more flexible now than they ever had before. We find business owners need to commit to more training and development of their workforce. More traditional apprenticeship programs need to be developed as well as experienced-based learning directly at companies willing to satisfy their own workforce development needs.

What impact has the pandemic had on the financial services industry?

Keven Prather: The pandemic has changed people's urgency to get things done. Most of us have lost someone during the pandemic, and it came as a complete surprise. So it just kind of pushes the timetable up and makes people realize that they are better off planning sooner than later. You will need to exit your business at some point in time, whether you define what the exit looks like or nature defines it for you.

What mistakes do you help people avoid?

Keven Prather: The biggest one is waiting too long. People wait too long to get started with their planning. I once asked a very wise attorney when the optimal time frame was for someone to start planning. He said, "When they write out the first paycheck to an employee. That is when they ought to start planning for their eventual retirement or transition out of the business." If they don't start soon enough, the company's value starts to wane off, and they might not get what they want out of the business in the end. Planning ahead is a smart play.

Keven, what inspired you to get started in the financial services field?

Keven Prather: I'm a United States Coast Guard veteran. In that role, I was always there on someone else's "worst day of their life." I'm very honored to have saved lives and saved property. That theme of wanting to help others has been in my background from a very early age.

When I was introduced to financial services, I had no idea that it was a possibility for me to even enter into this industry. And it's worked out pretty well. At an AALU conference in Washington DC, the guest speaker was a national security advisor under George W. Bush. He mentioned that this baby boom generation transfer is a major national security issue because it's a significant impact on our economy, as most businesses in the United States are privately held. And the baby boomers own all those businesses. They will leave, and what happens next is up to individuals to help those business owners plan. Most of America works for privately-held businesses. That's a fact. You know, I do believe that the United States is the greatest country on Earth because we have a deeply ingrained sense of liberty and entrepreneurism. In America, we create wealth through private business, and that's worth fighting for. It's worth preserving, and we find most business owners need some help in that preservation and stewardship of wealth.

What should people look for when choosing an advisor?

Keven Prather: This is where a little bit of gray hair might help. Is there a team behind the individual? Do they have the proper perspective? We take the philosophy of acting in the best interest of the business. If we work in the business's best interest, we serve the shareholders and the stakeholders. So ask about their philosophies and approaches to planning. Is it the core of what they do? Every time I think about doing something different, I get pulled back into working with business owners. Specialization is essential in this field because there is a lot to know. There is nobody who is an expert overall, but I would say that we are really good at being the orchestra conductors. So you might want to ask yourself, "Who is the conductor of the orchestra in my planning process?" These broad questions will give you a good sense of who you are dealing with.

How can people find you, connect with you, and learn more?

Keven Prather: Our website is www.transitionextadvisors.com. If you are looking for third-party validation, you can find me through the Business Enterprise Institute of Denver, Colorado. I am a member of BEI, and it is an excellent organization of professionals from all across the country. We work with businesses in every region of the country, so you can call the office at 440-895-7515 and talk to Kathy to set up a phone call with one of us. It all starts with a simple conversation.

KEVEN PRATHER, CFBS

Founder

TransitioNext Advisors

Keven is the founder of TransitioNext Advisors, a specialty firm that serves the complex needs of business owners through Financial Planning and Business Transition/Exit Planning. He enjoys working closely with business owners and their key employees to plan for the eventual transfer of ownership and control so that business owners can achieve their long-term goals. Using a Total Wealth Planning approach, TransitioNext Advisors' objective is to turn complex problems into actionable, understandable, and manageable steps by collaborating with business owners, their families, and strategic partners. We take a unique approach to help owners manage businesses as an "Asset Class" of investment. He addresses the question, "What have you done to prepare for the single largest financial transaction you will experience in your lifetime? That is the sale or transfer of control of your business." He plans for "Sales to Third Parties" or "Sales to Insiders," where the owner is no longer active in the business. Family dynamics and considerations are always critical in managing wealth. He integrates the owners' goals while preserving family harmony and legacies, which are all important parts of his overall service.

Keven is a graduate of the University of Idaho with a B.S. in Fisheries Resources. He is a member of the Phi Kappa Tau National Fraternity. He served as Domain Director for 15 years and served on the Host Committee for the Phi Kappa Tau National Convention in Cleveland, Ohio, in 2018. Keven served with distinction in the United States Coast Guard from 1986 to 1991 and continues to support the USCG in many ways through his community involvement. He was a founding member of the Lake County, Ohio Farmland Preservation Taskforce, a past Board Member for the USO of Northern Ohio, Community Liaison for Services to Armed Forces American Red Cross, and current Vice Chairman of the USS Cleveland Legacy Foundation. Professionally, Keven is a Certified Family Business Specialist (CFBS) and holds a certificate in Business Succession Planning from the American College. He is also a member of the Business Enterprise Institute (BEI) Network of Exit Planning Professionals™, the Financial Planning Association of Northeast Ohio, Society of Financial Service Professionals, Private Directors Association (PDA), and the Association for Corporate Growth (ACG). Keven is a certified Galliard Group Family Business Advisor and is an approved provider for Ohio Continuing Education (CPE) for CPAs. He is also a member of Services to the Armed Forces – American Red Cross.

WEBSITE: www.transitionextadvisors.com

PHONE: 440-895-7515

EMAIL: kprather@financialguide.com

ZACHARY MORRIS

ZACHARY MORRIS, CFP®

Conversation with Zachary Morris, CFP®

Zach, you are the Co-Founder of Paces Ferry Wealth Advisors out of Atlanta, Georgia. Tell us about your work and the people you help.

Zachary Morris: We started Paces Ferry Wealth Advisors in 2018 and became registered with the U.S Securities and Exchange Commission ("SEC"). Before that, my partner and I were with JP Morgan, and being at a big firm for a while, we decided we could provide a better client experience by starting our own company. So in 2018, we hit the ground running and transitioned many clients from our previous firm. The people we work with are asking themselves the questions, "Am I doing everything I should to set myself up for retirement? Am I on track?" We put together a complete financial plan for each client, showing them the path to retirement and what that looks like.

Has the pandemic changed how people think about financial planning?

Zachary Morris: I think people's mindsets have changed somewhat, though I don't think they should have. At the end of the day, I believe steady hands prevail. Anytime we have a crisis; generally, people's expectations are lower. They say, "If I could just get X percent, or I could just get Y percent." As people get more comfortable, they may start expecting more and more. But if people stick to their plans, continue to save, and don't take more risk than they need to hit their goals, they should do well through any type of environment, post-pandemic or not.

What are the most common concerns of your clients?

Zachary Morris: The biggest concerns are similar to pre-pandemic. Am I doing everything correctly to meet my retirement goals? Am I saving enough? Am I taking enough risk? Many people focus on the risk aspect of their investments. They think that if they just took more risk, they would be able to hit their goals quicker, and they'd be able to retire when they want to. But generally, what we're able to find when we put together a complete financial plan for somebody is that they can take less risk and still hit their goals.

Are there misconceptions surrounding financial planning?

Zachary Morris: The biggest misconception may involve how people should invest their money and how much risk they should take. I believe the industry has really led people to think they should invest to their maximum risk tolerance. People often ask the same question ten different ways to figure out how much risk they could tolerate, and very little focus is given to their actual goals.

People are usually led to believe that they should invest to their maximum risk tolerance, and if those investments do well, they can change their standard of living when they reach retirement. The problem with that approach is that most people are planning their retirement for ten, twenty, sometimes even thirty years, and they most likely have a pretty established idea of their desired standard of living. They have values, personalities, habits, and spending patterns to match them. So, why should someone invest their money to a maximum threshold of pain if it's unnecessary to reach their goals unless they have aspirations to be the richest guy in the graveyard? They should put more emphasis on their goals and only take a certain amount of risk necessary to reach those goals. We find that when clients benchmark "success" on their ability to achieve their goals, they are able to invest with more confidence, and the outcomes are typically more meaningful.

Another big misconception I see is that financial planning is a one-shot deal. Often when we speak to a potential new client, they have not updated a financial plan in many years. They haven't revisited their previous goals, added new goals, or updated the plan to match their current standard of living. The downside of this situation is that investors lose focus on why they are investing in the first place. They forget the purpose behind their investments and what they aim to accomplish with that money. This can sometimes lead to the investor taking on more risk than they might be comfortable with because they feel like they need to get higher returns to retire at some point in the future. Losing sight of their purpose for investing might lead them to hold future savings in cash due to uncertainty in the market, or they might even spend more money instead of saving because they don't feel comfortable investing.

What mistakes do you help your clients avoid?

Zachary Morris: People often fall into the trap of chasing the next hot thing. When your everyday investor hears about something on the news and all the big firms talk about it, they may think it is the best time to invest. In reality, that is typically the worst time to invest in something like that. The big firms usually offer something called "sell-side research," which tends to publish research based on the current trends and is very seldom predictive of what's to come. Most people remember late 2010 and early 2011 when most big firms talked about commodities as a necessity to hedge inflation in portfolios. This call to action was followed by a ten-year decline in the price of commodities. A few years later, in 2014, they rode the wave of the new era of the industrial revolution and the oil boom, just before oil started its six-year decline. They publish information based on what's popular and exciting at the time. They follow the momentum of the public psyche because it's easier to sell investments on a popular idea. We help clients understand the power of compounding, the value in steady returns, and a focus on long-term savings, which, while it may not be the most exhilarating concept, history has shown to be effective in the long run.

What advice would you give investors and savers to help set them up for success in their financial lives?

Zachary Morris: At the risk of sounding cliche, I would have to start with "live below your means." I have met millionaires that make $150k a year, and I have met thousandaires that make $650k. The consistent traits I find among wealthy individuals do NOT include excellent market timing, exciting stories of investment success, or get-rich-quick schemes. The characteristics I have seen are patience, hard work, and self-discipline. And most of the wealthy individuals live below their means. It's easy to get caught up in the idea that we have another paycheck coming, so why shouldn't we spend this one? We give ourselves a free pass once and then twice until it becomes a habit and ultimately a lifestyle. It might start out by trying to please the ones we love or to keep up with our neighbors, and then we set expectations that we feel must be maintained. Otherwise, we risk looking as though we are no longer successful. Unfortunately, maintaining our image is often at the expense of our personal goals. My advice is to strive to be anonymously rich and don't allow yourself to set any kind of expectations among your friends, family, or neighbors.

When people think about saving, they tend to get caught up in the idea of budgeting, get turned off by the whole concept, and ultimately abandon it altogether. You don't have to count pennies, stop buying Starbucks, and eat spaghetti every night to be a good saver. Living below your means could be as simple as buying a car that is $10,000 less rather than stretching to $10,000 more, doing one renovation a year instead of two, not giving gifts to each adult child each year, but instead just gifting them money as they need it and keeping track. Living below your means doesn't mean abandoning the things you love; it just means being more thoughtful in your spending on the other things.

What inspired you to get started in the financial services industry?

Zachary Morris: After I graduated from college, I worked at a bank for a year. And then, after that, I took off and traveled the world for six months, intending to come back and work in this industry. Unfortunately, when I came back, it was the middle of 2008. And it was a bad time to enter the field. So I worked for a startup company for three years, and then I met my current partner, Jeff Diamond, at JP Morgan.

I've always had an interest in finance. I always knew that I wanted to be successful. And so, I majored in finance because I wanted to have a good understanding of money. Eventually, I learned that I really enjoyed investing, teaching, and helping people, and I realized I could make a career out of it.

What should people look for when choosing a financial advisor?

Zachary Morris: One of the most important questions to ask is whether or not they are a fiduciary. Typically, the big firms adhere to something called the suitability standard of care. If it's suitable for the individual, they will buy it for them. The problem is, an investment can be suitable for an investor based on their age, net worth, and even risk tolerance. Often, a portfolio designed to be invested based on someone's maximum risk tolerance may be considered suitable, but it doesn't necessarily mean that it is in the client's best interest. It's knowing what is going on in the client's life and taking a more comprehensive view of not only their investment portfolio but their whole financial plan.

How can people find you, connect with you, and learn more?

Zachary Morris: Our website is www.pacesferrywealth.com.

You can also view many of our videos on YouTube. But if you want to contact me directly, my number is 404-480-5059. My email address is zmorris@pacesferrywealth.com.

ZACHARY MORRIS, CFP®

Wealth Advisor and Co-Founder

Paces Ferry Wealth Advisors

Having traveled to over 35 countries, Zach believes in Ralph Waldo Emerson's statement, *"Life is about the journey, not the destination."* Being a CERTIFIED FINANCIAL PLANNER™ provides Zach the opportunity to help clients define and realize their journey, and co-founding Paces Ferry Wealth Advisors, an independent firm, allows the freedom to establish the client experience along the way.

Previously, Zach was a partner in The Diamond Morris Group and a Financial Advisor with J.P. Morgan Securities, a wealth management division of J.P. Morgan. Before becoming a Financial

Advisor, Zach started as an Associate with the firm in 2011, where he developed skills for building lasting relationships with clients. Later, Zach developed and oversaw a training and mentorship program for J.P. Morgan Associates.

Zach received a B.S. in finance, with a minor in economics, from Elon University in North Carolina. He was a member of The Kappa Alpha Order and has served on the Elon Alumni Association's Atlanta chapter board. Zach speaks Spanish and is an Atlanta native. He, his wife, and their two kids live in West Midtown's Underwood Hills neighborhood in Atlanta, and his parents and two of his three sisters and their families live nearby. Zach golfs, plays tennis, rides his mountain bike, and travels in his spare time.

WEBSITE: www.pacesferrywealth.com

EMAIL: zmorris@pacesferrywealth.com

PHONE: 404-480-5059

SAMANTHA N. DINH

SAMANTHA N. DINH, CFP®

Conversation with Samantha N. Dinh, CFP®

Samantha, you are the Founder and CEO of Paragon Financial Planning. Tell us about your work and the people you help.

Samantha N. Dinh: I am a CERTIFIED FINANCIAL PLANNER™ registered with the CFP® Board and a fiduciary, which means that I am always obligated to act and recommend what is in the best interest of my clients. I specialize in helping entrepreneurs, C-suite executives, women, the tech industry, pre-retirees, and retirees create financial solutions to help them make more money and pay less in taxes while protecting themselves and the people they love most. Our holistic financial planning and wealth management process involves three steps: First, understanding our client's most important goals, where they have been financially, where they are now, and where they want to be in the future. Second, analyzing all of the strengths and weaknesses in their financial lives, the pros and cons of all options available, and developing strategies to help them get to their goals with the least amount of taxes in the most time-efficient manner. Third, we help clients implement their financial plan, manage their wealth, and make necessary changes as the economic, political, and health environment changes around them.

How has the recent pandemic impacted the financial services industry?

Samantha N. Dinh: The impact of the pandemic has created a heightened sense of urgency with regards to Financial Planning. Financial planning has always been around, but when we are faced with our own mortality, it forces us to think about what would happen to my family and the people I love if I was no longer here tomorrow? People are now more concerned with understanding where they stand financially, if they have enough life insurance, who would receive their assets, and how to construct their estate plan so that more can go to their loved ones and less to taxes, as well as making sure they have enough money for their families future once they are no longer here. It's a lot to think about, and I completely understand why all these questions keep them up at night, especially with the current pandemic. Our mission is to help our clients plan and execute so that all these questions are answered to have peace of mind now.

Are there common myths and misconceptions that prevent people from planning?

Samantha N. Dinh: We often hear people say, "I don't know if I have enough money to retire, or I am not sure if what I am doing is right." But whether you are starting from scratch or a multimillionaire, you can implement advice and financial planning tidbits to take a step forward to improve your financial life. The main thing is realizing where you are and where you want to be in the future. If you don't know where you're at, it will be very challenging to understand how to get to where you want to go. There is always a strategy to help you improve your finances. In my 20+ years, I have never met anyone who didn't benefit from implementing a new strategy as tax laws and the markets are always fluid.

How can people stay on track when it comes to financial planning?

Samantha N. Dinh: People should know how much they are making in income and, more importantly, how much they are really spending. It's important to know where the money is coming from, but it is even more important to know where it is going. Once you know your positive or negative cash flow, you can use it to fund your future financial goals. For example, you can reduce a little discretionary spending so that you can put money towards a life insurance policy to protect your family or reduce your taxes with a tax-advantaged retirement plan. If your budget and cash flow are tight, look at where you can cut back. The most common places are food and entertainment. For example, coffee and boba teas are really popular in the Bay Area right now, but you may want to cut some of those tasty drinks out and put that money towards a 401k. Minor tweaks can make a big difference in the long run.

What mistakes do you help your clients avoid?

Samantha N. Dinh: Don't leave any money on the table. If you're working for a company and they have an employer match, make sure that you put in at least enough to get that free money from the employer match. Ideally, if you have the positive cash flow available, you should try to make the maximum 401k contributions. In 2022, the maximum limits are going up to $20,500, which is a lot of tax savings. If you have your own business, there are many retirement plans available to help you reduce the tax burden as well. Our job is to know the rules of the game to help you win with the odds in your favor.

What inspired you to get started in the financial services field?

Samantha N. Dinh: Growing up, I always wanted to become a lawyer watching the People's Court and the many court tv shows at that time. I was actually on my way to law school after graduating with my bachelor's degree in economics and a minor in communications. My brother is a very successful attorney in SF, and many of my current clients are attorneys. However, I realized that I loved helping people solve problems in win-win situations where my clients could succeed, I could succeed, and I could do just that in other career spaces outside of law. I have always been exceptionally good at problem-solving and thinking outside the box to get to the end goal. I am also an avid lifelong learner who thrives on finding creative ways to navigate the nuances of life. So I thought, "What can I do to utilize all of my skills and passions to fulfill my life's purpose?" I went through many job fairs out of college, and when I saw financial planning, I thought, "Oh my gosh, that makes perfect sense." Coming from an Asian background, the only careers that really existed were doctors, engineers, and lawyers. So when I approached my parents and told them I was going to be a financial planner instead of an attorney, they thought I was nuts! But after 20 plus years of being a part of all of life's ups and downs with our clients, helping them make more informed decisions for themselves, their businesses, and their families, it has truly been very rewarding financially and, more importantly, personally. The valuable long-term relationships we have with our clients have been instrumental in serving my life's purpose.

If you could communicate with your younger self, what advice would you share?

Samantha N. Dinh: That's a great question, and I have many things I would love to share with my younger self, but I'll keep it to financial advice only. I would tell my younger self to stick to the three most important rules- PSI. 1. Plan 2. Save 3. Invest. First, always start a plan with the end in mind - most people don't plan to fail; they just fail to plan. When you have a plan, you can understand the big picture, map out the optimal paths to your goals, and pivot when you are off track. Second, save for an emergency fund and establish a positive monthly cash flow. Cash flow is the difference between how much income is generated vs. how much you are spending. The long-term rewards are so much better when you can delay your gratification. When you have a positive cash flow, you can fund your future goals of retirement, college, or a home purchase. Life is all about needs and wants, so spend your money on needs first and decide what you can afford to spend on your wants after. Moderation is key. Ideally, you should also have at least six months of emergency funds for monthly expenses in an easy-to-access bank account. Lastly, investing your positive monthly cash flow and any extra money that you have above your six months of emergency fund in a diversified portfolio for the long term will enable you to reach your goals sooner. Did you know that your money only needs to double 20 times to turn $1 into 1 million dollars?!? Try it; if you started with $1, how many times would you need to double your money until it becomes $1 million? Using that same example, if your investment portfolio made 7% per year, then your portfolio should double every ten years. This should give everyone hope that you, too, can become a millionaire with the right plan, effort, and guidance.

What should people look for when choosing a financial advisor?

Samantha N. Dinh: I would highly recommend choosing a CERTIFIED FINANCIAL PLANNER™ who is registered with the CFP® board, who is also a fiduciary, and someone you can see yourself having a long-term relationship with. Interview at least three advisors and pick the one who can convey complex concepts in simple terms. You don't want anyone to talk over you. You want someone who is like a friend giving you advice, "Here are the pros, here are the cons. Here is what I would do." A good financial advisor should help guide you and be a resource of invaluable information to better you and your family's lives.

How can people find you, connect with you, and learn more?

Samantha N. Dinh: My website is www.paragon-fp.com. Our direct office telephone number is 510-227-5354, and we are located in the San Francisco Bay Area in California. We would love to connect with you.

SAMANTHA N. DINH, CFP®

Certified Financial Planner™

Paragon Financial Planning, Inc.

Samantha N. Dinh is a Certified Financial Planner™ and has been in the financial services industry for more than 20 years. Samantha's focus is to help her clients make, protect, and transfer their money to their loved ones and to the causes that they believe in so they can live a life of significance that they have envisioned for themselves and their families. After more than 14 years at a Wall Street Firm, Samantha went on to create an independent private practice in the San Francisco Bay Area to better provide unbiased advice and service to individuals, women, business owners, the tech industry, pre-retirees/retirees, and their families. Her services include retirement planning, stock equity optimization strategies, investment strategic planning, estate planning, risk management, and tax minimization planning.

Samantha is married, and her son, Sean, and daughter, Sage, are the apples of her eye, besides her husband, of course. She enjoys traveling, eating, and learning about all cultures, cuisines, and languages of the world. She is an avid plant mommy to many fruit trees, including eight types of guavas, passion fruit, and papaya, to name a few, and many varieties of houseplant babies.

Samantha graduated from the University of California at Davis with a Bachelor of Science in Managerial Economics with an emphasis in Financial Management and a minor in Communications. She has seven professional registrations, which include the series seven held through LPL Financial, series 66 held through Strategic Wealth Advisors Group LLC and LPL Financial, California insurance license, California Long Term Care, California Partnership for Long Term Care, the AAMS® (Accredited Asset Management Specialist), and the CFP® (Certified Financial Planner).

WEBSITE: www.paragon-fp.com

PHONE: 510-227-5354

ABOUT THE PUBLISHER

Mark Imperial is a Best-Selling Author, Syndicated Business Columnist, Syndicated Radio Host, and internationally recognized Stage, Screen, and Radio Host of numerous business shows spotlighting leading experts, entrepreneurs, and business celebrities.

His passion is to discover noteworthy business owners, professionals, experts, and leaders who do great work and share their stories and secrets to their success with the world on his syndicated radio program titled "Remarkable Radio."

Mark is also the media marketing strategist and voice for some of the world's most famous brands. You can hear his voice over the airwaves weekly on Chicago radio and worldwide on iHeart Radio.

Mark is a Karate black belt; teaches Muay Thai and Kickboxing; loves Thai food, House Music, and his favorite TV shows are infomercials.

Learn more:

www.MarkImperial.com
www.BooksGrowBusiness.com

Made in the USA
Monee, IL
04 November 2026

67376107R00069